Sermons For Pentecost I Based On Gospel Texts For Cycle C

The Chain Of Command

Alexander H. Wales

D1374065

CSS Publishing Company, Inc., Lima, Ohio

SERMONS FOR PENTECOST I BASED ON GOSPEL TEXTS FOR CYCLE C:
THE CHAIN OF COMMAND

Copyright © 1997 by
CSS Publishing Company, Inc.
Lima, Ohio

Some scripture quotations are from the *Revised Standard Version of the Bible*, copy-
righted 1946, 1952 ©, 1971, 1973, by the Division of Christian Education of the National
Council of the Churches of Christ in the USA. Used by permission.

Some scripture quotations are from the *Good News Bible*, in Today's English Version.
Copyright © American Bible Society 1966, 1971, 1976. Used by permission.

Library of Congress Cataloging-in-Publication Data

Wales, Alexander H., 1948-
    Sermons for Pentecost I based on Gospel texts for cycle C : the chain of command /
Alexander H. Wales.
        p.   cm.
    ISBN 0-7880-1047-6 (pbk.)
    1. Pentecost season—Sermons.   2. Bible. N.T. Gospels—Sermons.   3. Sermons,
American. I. Title. II. Title: Sermons for Pentecost 1 based on Gospel texts for cycle C.
III. Title: Sermons for Pentecost one based on Gospel texts for cycle C.   IV. Title: Hom-
ing in on the heart.
BV61.W35   1997
252'.64—DC21   96-46496
                                                                                                            CIP

This book is available in the following formats, listed by ISBN:
        0-7880-1047-6   Book
        0-7880-1048-4   Mac
        0-7880-1049-2   IBM 3 1/2
        0-7880-1094-8   Sermon Prep

*To Barbara,
Emily & Nathan*

Editor's Note Regarding The Lectionary

During the past two decades there has been an attempt to move in the direction of a uniform lectionary among various Protestant denominations.

Preaching on the same scripture lessons every Sunday is a step in the right direction of uniting Christians of many faiths. If we are reading the same scriptures together, we may also begin to accomplish other achievements. Our efforts will be strengthened through our unity.

Beginning with Advent 1995 The Evangelical Lutheran Church in America dropped its own lectionary schedule and adopted the Revised Common Lectionary.

Reflecting this change, resources published by CSS Publishing Company put their major emphasis on the Revised Common Lectionary texts for the church year.

Table Of Contents

Preface

What you are about to experience is a variety of styles in sermoneering that represents many years of ministry, more than half of which were spent as a staff member and not as a preacher. I call it an "appelage," a word coined in a college dorm that described a host of things coming at you that took a while to put into perspective. That may be what you find in this collection of sermons.

There are first person monologues, short tales to prove a point, traditional "three point" manuscripts, and a style that has grown on its own. I would encourage you to add your own illustrations, comments, and study if you choose to use them "as is." Or perhaps they can be a jumping off point (and some of my critics have suggested that that is how some of my listeners respond to my preaching — although no deaths or serious injuries have been reported) for creative work of your own.

I have tried to present material that is not footnoted as I find scholarly dissertation a difficult process to present in a listener friendly manner. If there is something that needs to be added, I invite you to do so. More often than not, when I have quoted Scripture, it has come from the TEV Good News Bible, as I find it very "listenable" for the hearer without losing the biblical heritage to which it is rooted.

I hope you find the materials useful in letting the Spirit flow from you to your hearers, and that helpful or not, you will read it and discover ...

Peace,

Alex Wales

Show Us The Father

Pentecost   *John 14:8-17, 25-27*

This morning, I would like to take you on a little journey
with your imagination to meet someone who is a vital part of the
Christian story of faith. He appears in this morning's Gospel lesson, and I believe that he offers us a unique perspective upon our
Pentecost celebration. So, close your eyes and let this person tell
you about what he experienced.

"I didn't mean to get Jesus so mad at me that night. It had been
an exhausting evening and I didn't mean to push. By the way, my
name is Philip, and I am one of Jesus' closest friends and disciples.

"We had ridden into town on Sunday with such great expecta-
tions. Jerusalem was getting ready to celebrate Passover and was
full of people. The crowd had been so welcoming. It seemed as
though everyone was there. Shouts of 'Hosanna' filled the air. We
were greeted like visiting royalty. It was heady stuff for our first
day in the capital city.

"And then, there had been that confrontation at the Temple.
Jesus had thrown the money changers out. I'd never seen him so
angry. With that rope swinging around his head and the temple
officials running for cover, he reminded me of one of the old-time
prophets spewing out the wrath of God. I think they got his message, but I also knew that he had made some more enemies as well.

9

"Then, we spent some time with him preaching about the coming of the Kingdom. I knew that something was bothering him, but he'd been rather moody ever since he and Peter and John had gone up to the top of that mountain, kind of lost in thought, thinking about other things. Peter claimed that Moses and Elijah had been there, that Jesus had glowed with a special light. But you know that Peter, always getting so involved that his mouth is in gear long before his brain starts working.

"Anyway, when Jesus finished with the crowds, he spent some quiet time with us disciples. He was talking about what was going to happen, but none of us really understood what he meant. Then, he told us about eating together in the upper room at the home of Josiah.

"That day, he had some of us go and make arrangements for the meal, but you know, it was as though he had already made plans before we got to Jerusalem. There was a man carrying a water jug who seemed to know all about what we were going to do that night. I went ahead and paid for the room and the caterer, just like I always did. You see, I was in charge of the funds we used. All the disciples just put money into the bag I carried as they got it from people who wanted to help us in our ministry. That was an important responsibility, but Jesus knew I could do a good job. My mother always said I had a good head for numbers.

"When evening came, we went to the house and headed upstairs. Jesus started things off by washing our feet. He was always doing things like that. Kept trying to teach us about being servants of God and others. It was really embarrassing having someone as important as Jesus doing something so common. Peter wasn't even going to let Jesus do it, but Jesus insisted.

"Jesus also told Peter that night that he was going to deny him. We all snickered at that. Peter was always so sure of himself. If we had known that all of us would do the same thing, it wouldn't have seemed so funny. That was when Jesus told us that one of us would betray him, but we couldn't believe that one of us would do anything like that. When Judas left, we didn't even notice.

"It was after that when Jesus began teaching again. Most of us weren't listening very carefully. I mean, we were full after a big meal and the room was warm. First, Peter got into it with Jesus. That's when Jesus told Peter about the rooster crowing after Peter would say that he didn't know Jesus. Then, Thomas got into it by asking where Jesus was going and how we didn't know how to get there.

"When Jesus said he was the way, the truth, and the life, it didn't mean much to me. Jesus had always been important to us. I just didn't know he was the way that he would prove to be. I also didn't realize how upset Jesus was that we were all being so dense in understanding what he was telling us.

"When I asked him to show us the Father, I was just trying to tell him how hard it was for us to believe that we were doing God's work. After all those months, all those people, all those healings, it seemed that people were still not able to understand what we were doing. I guess that it was true, even for us. We were with him every day, but we didn't understand. We saw, but we didn't really. We listened but only caught a small portion of what he was teaching. It would be years before we really began to understand so much of what he had said.

"So, I made what I thought was an obvious request. If Jesus could only show us a little glimpse of God, then we would have been able to be sure that we were on the right track. I didn't realize how stupid I would feel when he responded.

" 'You mean, Philip, that you have been with me all these months and you have the audacity to ask me that! I have been with you all and still, you don't know me! If you've seen me, you've seen the Father, Philip. Don't you realize that I am in the Father, and my Father is in me?

" 'All the things I have been saying don't come from me. The Father has been in me doing his own work. Believe me when I say that I am in the Father and the Father is in me. And if you can't believe what I'm saying, at least believe because of the things you have seen me do. If you believe in me, you will do even greater things, because I am going to the Father. I will do whatever you ask for in my name, so the Father's glory will be shown through me. If you ask for anything in my name, I will do it.'

"Looking back, I can't believe how dense I was. I didn't understand what he was saying to us. Here was Jesus telling us plainly that he was the chosen one, and we thought we understood that. Why, we didn't have the foggiest!

"Of course, after his crucifixion, most of us gave up hope. It wasn't until Sunday morning that we even had the faintest inkling of what he had meant. When the women came that day to say he was risen, we had forgotten all about his being one with the Father. You would have thought we had never even met him, much less have lived with him all those months.

"And then when he ascended, we were lost again. I don't know why we couldn't remember what he had said. But it slowly came back to us. We remembered his promise of the Holy Spirit that would guide us and keep us safe. We thought we were alone. We sat in that upper room with the door locked, sure that we would never see him again. We were like a bunch of lost kids, no leader, no direction, no real reason to remain there except that Jesus had told us to wait.

"And then it came. On that Pentecost day, the Holy Spirit came to us and it was like seeing for the first time. His words rang sure and true. The reality of who Jesus was was as clear as crystal. All the fog lifted. It felt like I could see all the way to eternity. We suddenly knew that Jesus was inside each and every one of us.

"Jesus promised us that we would have a helper to get us through this time. He also promised us a peace that we had never known. We got it that day. After all the turmoil, all the fear, all the confusion, when the Spirit came to us that day in Jerusalem, every doubt, every question, every struggle faded away. To be touched by God's power in such an incredible way — there's no describing it. My anxiety was gone. I knew that I didn't have to worry about anything. Even my greatest fears seemed to subside. In one sense, I was as naked as a newborn baby. But at the same moment, I knew I was clothed in the most beautiful, most secure, most indestructible clothing I had ever possessed.

"I remember running around that day, jabbering to anyone who would listen. I was just bubbling over with joy, ecstatic at being in the presence of God. I remember the others who were just as overcome by God's goodness and light. They were just as giddy as I was.

"There was power everywhere. People were being healed. People were proclaiming God's goodness, offering God praise. It was as though we were all drunk. I know that's what other people claimed, but it was true. We were filled to overflowing with God's spirit. It was magnificent.

"I'm only sorry that I didn't see the Father sooner. There I was in the presence of God all that time, and I was blind. If I had just looked, I would have seen God during the time we traveled around Judea, but I needed the Holy Spirit to help me see.

"If there's anything I could wish for you, it would be that you, too, would find the Spirit of God descending upon you like a dove out of heaven. It happens all the time. Just tell God that you're ready. Jesus promised that it would come. Believe me. I'm one who knows."

So Much To Say,
So Little Time

The Holy Trinity   *John 16:12-15*

The hours were passing rapidly. Time was running out. Jesus was trying to get everything in order for what he knew was to be the end of his ministry. He had so much to say, and yet, he was aware of the fact that the disciples were just not ready to take it all in.

Up to this point, they were struggling just to understand what he had been trying to tell them. They were still stumbling over the meaning of the parables, attempting to put some flesh on stories that seemed to be like a gossamer cloth spun with gold thread, yet impossible to grasp even when they had their hands on it.

They were constantly bickering with each other, trying to get a more prominent place in the order of things, a little like first graders lining up at the water fountain at school. For twelve grown men, you'd think that they would have been more sophisticated, but we have to remember that these were commoners, men of passions, used to living lives of intensity on fishing boats, on farms, in workshops, and in tax offices. They were the blue-collar workers of their time, skilled and yet not educated, used to the basics, not interested in what the future might hold because they found life difficult enough in the present.

In other words, the disciples were like you and me. Our educational levels might be different, our cultural experiences might

15

lead us to believe that we "know" more, but when it comes down to living day to day, we are not so far apart. Jesus was trying to talk to a group of people who could be sitting in this room at this very moment right alongside of us.

Jesus wanted to speak to his disciples in a clear and direct manner. But how could he expect them to hear all that they needed to hear with so little time left? The more he spoke about the future, the more fear and anxiety filled their minds and faces.

Did you ever notice how it gets harder to hear when someone is telling you something you do not want to hear? Like when the doctor comes in with test results that you have been dreading. Or when your boss calls you in to tell you about some restructuring that is going to have to take place. Or when the principal asks for a special conference about the report card that is about to be distributed. You would think that would be the time when you could focus in and increase your ability to listen. Instead, we tend to get fuzzier and more confused. I have a feeling that is what Jesus could see in the disciples' faces as they listened around the table in that upper room.

Then Jesus offers something new, something entirely different, something that would ease the confusion and soothe the furrowed brows of the disciples. He tells them that the Spirit will lead them into the truth. The Spirit will speak with the authority of God, telling the disciples what God wants said to them. The Spirit will give Jesus glory because he will translate what Jesus has to say to the disciples. Jesus tells them that he possesses all that the Father has. Jesus and God are one.

In that one instant of declaration, we have the Trinity — Father, Son and Spirit, different and yet the same, speaking the word of God, being the Word of God and enabling the word of God to become inextricably bound with the disciples. And, in all likelihood, the disciples missed it.

They were still caught up in what Jesus had said about what was going to happen, what he had said about himself, about how the world was going to treat them because of their relationship with him. They heard, but they didn't understand. "Let him who has ears, hear," as Jesus had said so often.

Perhaps the meal had slowed down their reflexes, the same way that a thanksgiving feast affects us. Everything had gone into slow motion. Jesus was talking in those theological terms that always got them so confused. They really didn't want to get into any deep reflection upon what the future might hold. Of course, they didn't know that the future was going to be very different in just a few short hours.

Yet they were concerned. There was enough being said that they knew that things were about to be different. Jesus was promising them that there would be someone around to help make the confusion clear. That they weren't expecting the Spirit is clear in the Pentecost story. The Spirit brings clarity and power, but no one is ready for what would happen.

Two thousand years later, the church isn't much different. We are still confused by the theological implications of a God made flesh on earth. We still stumble around when we try to put faith into action. We still need the constant presence of the Spirit to make sense of our faith. And we still are surprised every time the Spirit comes into our lives to make us truly God's children.

How many of us here would be ready if God's Spirit were to pour into this room and make us into someone that we didn't want to be, or make us do something we really were not ready to do? Most of us would like to believe that we would be ready, but if it really happened ... I'm not sure. You see, we are not sure we want to trust God that much.

What would happen if God tried to tell us something different from what we thought we already knew? Remember, that's what happened to Paul on the road to Damascus. Paul was riding to that city to rid it of those Christians who were threatening his Jewish faith. He had no intention of letting that group of religious upstarts upset the boat of faith that he was sailing on. He had the compass. He knew the waters. He was involved in smooth sailing, when suddenly, that whirlwind known as Jesus had something more to say to him. Knocked him right off his horse! Upset his apple cart and made applesauce of his pretensions! Left him blind and in the hands of the very people he was intent on stopping.

You see, when Jesus has more to say, he is going to find a way to say it. The Spirit is the venue, the media that carries the message right to the heart of the one he wants to speak to. We have to be fairly smug if we believe that we are somehow going to stop his message from getting through to us.

Jesus has so much to say and we have so little time to listen to all that he wants to teach us. It was true with the disciples. It continues to be true with us. We intend to listen. We are determined to be faithful followers. But the moment we hear his voice, we begin to get anxious. His words pour down upon us like a shower, and we worry about getting wet rather than seeking to understand. He speaks about eternal things and we are caught up in the present.

We still need someone to speak to us in a different manner, someone who will help us hear and believe in spite of our disbelief. We need the Spirit to be there, to help us to hear. But the Spirit does more than help us hear. The Spirit is active in guiding us in the truth. The Spirit is power and potential and personality that make us shine out in a world filled with darkness. We become the bearers of the truth, marked by the reality of the Trinity — children of the Father, siblings of the Son, companions of the Spirit — so that all may hear and know the Good News of Jesus Christ. Amen.

The Chain Of Command

Proper 4   *Luke 7:1-10*
Pentecost 2
Ordinary Time 9

"When I spoke with the Rabbi about this itinerant preacher, Jesus, I knew right away that he was the one I would have to go to if Gaius was going to survive. Gaius has been with me since the campaigns against the barbarians in the north. He's probably the closest servant and friend I've ever had in all my years of military service. Knowing how sick he was, knowing that our doctors had done all they could, there wasn't really anywhere I could turn except for some miraculous cure.

"This Jesus fellow has been making quite a stir in these parts. I know that some of the people in power dislike him, but the common people are attracted to him. There are all sorts of claims that this Jesus has done miracles. Some even say he walks on water, but I know that some of Rome's enemies think that the Legion walks on water. I haven't seen anything with my own eyes to tell you one way or the other.

"I figured that the best way to get to Jesus was to go through some of the temple and synagogue leaders. They're divided on how they respond to Jesus, but they all have at least a grudging respect for him and his disciples. If anyone was going to be able to speak to Jesus about Gaius, I assumed that they would.

19

"I've always had a good relationship with the Jewish religious leaders here in Judea. I am well aware of the fact that most of the Legion thinks of this area as the worst possible assignment, but if you can stand the dust and heat of the summer, the rest of the year is pleasant enough. And while the people can be a little overly zealous in their religious fervor, there is something about their faith that I find attractive. There's a purity, a feeling of purpose and morality that exists in Judaism that makes a lot of sense to me. It's like the military code that guides the Legion — follow the code and you're guaranteed a daily ration and a regular income. Sure, there are some dangers, but there are dangers everywhere. They seem to respect me, and I respect them.

"Anyway, they owed me something. A couple of years ago, I was able to get a work project done in this quarter of the city — had a synagogue built. The one they were meeting in was in bad shape. When I asked for their help, they responded quickly.

"At first, they were afraid that Jesus might not want to help, what with Gaius and me being Gentiles and all that. That's what they call us — Gentiles. Or if they're mad at us — pagans, although the word *Gentiles* seems to be a little less hostile. Actually, in their parlance, I'm probably considered a God-fearer. That's someone who not only respects their religious practices, but even is attracted to their faith. And I guess I am. Like I said, Judaism has some things that seem to make a lot of sense. They have a real respect for family, a little like we used to have in Rome, before all this empire stuff got started.

"Now, the politicians back home are using too much authority for my taste. Why, the emperor is even claiming to be divine! Of course, I've seen the emperors on the battlefield. I know that they can be wounded, even die, just like any other man. I don't think that an imperial proclamation can make a man into a god, but then again, who am I to say?

"Jesus heard their pleas, because he started off towards my house. Gaius has been upstairs on the roof since he became ill. It's a little cooler up there when the breeze gets blowing. I could see the crowd coming this way from up there. I finally realized that Jesus wouldn't want to enter the house — him being a religious leader, and me being a Gentile. This house would be unclean to him, especially with Gaius being so sick. I had one of the servant girls go and tell him not to trouble himself by coming all the way here. I knew that I wasn't worthy enough to have him come this far out of his way.

"I realized that if this man can do what they claim he can do, he didn't have to come here to make Gaius well. I've lived my whole life around authority. I can take orders just as well as give them. If he could turn water into wine, feed a crowd of 5,000, and make blind men see, then all he'd have to do is say the word and it would be done! If you have authority, you can make anything happen. When the emperor in Rome tells us to march, we march! If Jesus is as close to the Jewish God as they say he is, he could do the same thing.

"And he did! I knew the moment he healed Gaius. He said it, and it happened. Gaius was lying there, burning up with fever. Then, all of a sudden, the fever was gone and Gaius began to be like himself again. Why, before evening had come Gaius was scurrying around the house, getting things in order as though he had never been sick. You would never have known that he had been lying at death's door just hours before.

"But I just knew Jesus could do it. There were too many people around who believed that he had a special relationship with God, too many to ignore. You see, I'm a simple man when you get right down to it. You either have power or you don't. People who are con artists always have some people who have their doubts. But I never met anyone who had met Jesus who didn't believe that he had some special relationship with God. That's why I knew he could heal Gaius. He could and he did! I thank God for sending Jesus my way. That's all there is to it."

Luke tells us the story of a Roman soldier who has a special experience with Jesus. He's a soldier who knows authority when he sees it: a military man who also knew power from both sides of the fence. He knew that Jesus had power, and that if he chose to use it, he could perform miracles. It was not a matter of hoping and wishing. It was a practical understanding of an apparent truth. This Roman soldier had faith in the fact that Jesus was who he claimed to be. Jesus recognized the incredible faith that this soldier had.

This Roman did not ask "why?" or "how?" or "for what purpose?" He knew that people believed that Jesus could do what he said he could do, and asked Jesus for help. It was that simple. He was aware of the chain of command that existed in the military establishment. He saw that same connection in the power of God. If that power of God was, then this soldier believed in what was.

Why is it so hard for us to have that kind of faith? Why is it that we need proof, need to see more than we do to believe? I think that part of our problem is that we are caught by our doubt and our inability to give up control. We want to know before we can believe. We want to see before we can walk. We do not like the idea that someone has that much control over us.

This Roman soldier lived his life as part of the chain of command. There were people above him and people below him. He was just one of the links. If he could be a strong link, then the chain would remain solid and he would be safe. He put his trust in that chain, and knew that if the others would do the same, the chain could maintain an empire.

Isn't it odd that we are part of a similar chain, one that speaks about a kingdom rather than an empire? And we are called to believe that all things are possible; that if we ask, we shall receive; that if we seek, we shall find; and if we knock, the door will be opened for us. What we need to do is understand the chain of command that we live in as the servants of the living Lord.

The Other Resurrection

Proper 5   *Luke 7:11-17*
Pentecost 3
Ordinary Time 10

If you ask most Christians who Jesus raised to life, the most common response you would get would be "Lazarus." How could we miss the story of the raising of the brother of Mary and Martha? The three days in the tomb caused the sisters to warn Jesus that Lazarus would "stinketh." What a great word, "stinketh"! It sounds like something you would say about a high school locker room after a big basketball game. The resurrection story found in the chapter 11 of the Gospel of John is THE story that springs to mind when we talk about the incredible power of Jesus even over the minions of death.

But here in chapter 7 of Luke, we have another miraculous resurrection of an individual without much fanfare or comment: a miracle that ranks right up there with walking on water and bringing sight to the blind, but which gets less than exciting press coverage. I have a feeling that we tend to leave it alone because we get embarrassed by it.

You see, this is a miracle without much explanation or theological intrigue. It happens so quickly that we read it, swallow hard and move on. Just think about how it all happens.

Jesus is continuing his itinerant preaching and teaching. He reaches the gates of the city of Nain, and you could read "Podunk" if you like. The disciples and a large crowd are with him as they notice a funeral procession heading out of town to the local cemetery. We are told by Luke that the person who had died was a widow's only son, although we don't know that anyone in the crowd knew that at the time. We do know that the woman was attended by a large crowd of villagers. Jesus saw the woman, and with pity for her, went up to her and told her not to cry.

Of course, that is not the best thing to say to someone who is grieving the loss of a loved one, unless you just happen to be able to take away the grief. Jesus walked over to the coffin and touched it, something that no Jew who would be concerned with staying ritually clean would do. His action caused the pallbearers to stop in their tracks.

Then, the miracle occurs. "Young man! Listen to me! Get up!"

The young man sat up and began talking. Before long, Jesus was returning him to his mother. One who had been dead was suddenly alive again.

Luke continues his story by telling us that the observers of this event were filled with fear and praised God. They recognized that a great prophet had come to be among them. The news about Jesus went out throughout the countryside.

That is the story. Concise and clear. But what's the point? Why did Jesus bring this young man back to life? What issues of faith were addressed? Was he resurrected because of his faith? Or his mother's faith? Did Jesus know him beforehand and therefore felt it necessary to step in? It seems like a spectacular miracle. Why does it get lost in the rest of the story? Why don't we find more people flocking to Jesus if he can turn the process of death around and make people live?

But as Paul Harvey says, "Here's the rest of the story." There is more going on here than meets the eye. First of all, we have the story taking place in the city of Nain. As I said, "Podunk, Judea" — a little nothing of a town whose greatest asset was a wall that protected it. It was also remembered that in that same area, in just about the same place, the prophet Elisha raised another woman's son. A little bit of deja vu, biblical style! The first resurrection story proved that Elisha truly was a prophet who had inherited the mantle of Elijah. In the second story, the people proclaim that there truly was a prophet in their midst. Jesus was repeating history that proved that God was in the process of saving God's holy people.

Secondly, we see Jesus comforting a widow at the death of her son. He stops her weeping and returns her son to the land of the living. Shades of Easter! There will be a widow who will see her son die, only to have her tears of sorrow replaced with tears of joy at the words on an early Sunday morning that declare: HE IS NOT HERE. HE IS RISEN! Again, we see the echo of another story resounding in the first.

And thirdly, we see a Jesus moved by compassion for someone in the deepest pain. Jesus is moved by this grieving widow and her sorrow at the loss of her son. We still must ask why Jesus is moved by this particular widow in this particular setting. Surely, he must have seen other funerals and other individuals in grief. Surely, he must have had opportunity to make this kind of incredible miracle happen in other places.

Perhaps it was the remoteness of Nain that let him act in such a dramatic manner. Nothing big ever happens in those small towns around the world. Just ask anyone from Knob Noster or Pinkersville. The teens in those towns will tell you that nothing big ever happens there. Why, some of those small one-horse towns have to close down when the horse dies!

Perhaps, Jesus saw his own mother in that widow — someone whose life had been centered around her children, who had faced the world alone, and who would have to face impossible pain at the death of her child. Maybe in this one instance, he could respond to the anguish that he saw so often in the world around him. He could not always deal with each individual's pain during his earthly ministry, but in this one instance maybe he was able to respond without having to make a theological statement for all the world to see.

The resurrection of this young man still makes us uncomfortable. There is nothing in Luke's discussion to give a hint about why Jesus chose to bring this man back to life. If not faith, if not to prove some theological understanding, if not to echo some of the Old Testament stories, if not to fulfill an Old Testament prophecy, why does this miracle take place?

Could it be to tell the disciples and us that God's grace is beyond our understanding? Could it be that it reminds us that there are things that God does that are beyond our human comprehension? Might it suggest that God will do things the way God wants to do things even though we might not agree? There are times when even those with the greatest faith and the surest comprehension find the will of God incomprehensible. Jesus could be moved by something he saw happen that touched his heart. He responded because he could respond — not because it was theologically sound, or because it would make greater numbers of followers, but because he could and he chose to do so.

So, we find a man lying in a hospital, wracked with pain from cancer, a hopeless case with no reason to hope, who suddenly, miraculously is healed — no sign of cancer, no scars of agony, nothing to explain the sudden health. He has received the same prayers, the same care as other patients in the same hospital, but he does not die when others do. Is it because he has lived a better life? Or been more faithful in his obedience? Or because he has some other purpose to fulfill before he dies? We do not, cannot, know. It lies within the providence of God. It is the result of God's unending grace.

Or we find a family pulled apart by hostility, abounding in infidelity, living beyond their means, when suddenly grace abounds and everything changes. The family survives and prospers. There is shock and amazement from all those who have witnessed the passing events. Why did it happen? What caused this change when others who so desperately wanted a similar result failed to have it? The ways of God are as mysterious as they have ever been. We can only thank God for the gift of grace.

Or we find individuals immersed in sin, unable to find a way out, when suddenly a savior comes who offers forgiveness when none is warranted. There is no reason for this grace except that love is the prevalent reality. We all have been in that funeral procession at some point in our lives. We have all been dead even though we have been going through the motions of life. And then, for some unfathomable reason, God steps in and brings us to life, offering the only begotten Son for our sake, as a sacrifice for our sinfulness. A resurrection has taken place. We are returned to our heavenly parent, who had thought us lost, and who rejoices in our return to life in all its glory.

Simply Simon

"I just don't understand the man! I invited him into my home and what do I get? INSULTS! He was a guest in my house. I don't think he understands who he's dealing with! Some people just can't be satisfied with what they've received. Let me explain ...

"You see, a few weeks back, I heard that Jesus of Nazareth was going to be in our area. You know, he's that roving preacher who's so popular with the public right now. In fact, I've heard he's done some amazing things during his meetings. And he teaches some good, Bible-based stuff, getting back to the basics, talking about the heart kind of religion rather than the rule bound religion that is so popular with the 'in' group nowadays. I've heard that he tends to step on some sensitive toes every once in a while, but I think that's always going to be true with some of these hard-liners.

"Anyway, when I heard he was going to be in town, I sent one of my servants to visit with his disciples to see if I could get him to eat at our house while he was here. Thought it would be good to have someone like him in the house, get to know him personally, hear his perspective on things. And it wouldn't be bad for my image, what with his popularity and all. So he accepted and I invited some of my friends over as well.

29

"Well, he arrived last Thursday night with all of his disciples. Can you imagine! Twelve of the scruffiest men you've ever seen — fishermen, laborers. Why, he even has a tax collector in that group! Not that I mind, though. I'm open to all kinds of people being part of the temple community. But I didn't know he'd bring all twelve of them. I thought the caterer was going to blow a gasket.

"We'd just gotten down to dinner when you would not believe who should walk in. There is a lady in town who has the worst reputation in the area. She has a police blotter as long as your arm. Anyway, she came in, right through the front door, carrying a jar of perfume. She went over to Jesus and began wiping his feet with her hair. In fact, I think she was crying, making this big fuss over him. Then she began pouring the perfume on his feet.

"I could not believe that she had the nerve to come into my house, let alone be bold enough to touch Jesus. And Jesus ... why, he never even said a word. It was so obvious what kind of woman she was, and Jesus just sat there letting her make a spectacle of herself. Makes my skin crawl just thinking about it!

"I was just about ready to have her thrown out of the house when Jesus spoke to me. He said, 'Simon, tell me: there were two men who owed money to a loan shark. One owed five hundred bucks and the other owed fifty. Neither of the two guys could pay, so the loan shark canceled the debts of both of them. Now, which one will love the loan shark more?'

"I had heard that Jesus was always putting people on the spot with his tricky questions, but this one was a no-brainer. 'I suppose the one who owed him the most,' I answered back.

"Jesus immediately confirmed my answer. 'Right you are, Simon!' But then he turned to the woman and said, 'Simon, do you see this woman? I came into your house as your guest, but you didn't offer me any water to wash my feet. She washed my feet with her tears and dried them with her hair. You didn't welcome me with a kiss, and all she seems to do is continue kissing my feet. You didn't provide any olive oil for my head after a weary day in the hot sun, but she has bathed my feet with perfume. The great love she has shown proves that her many sins have been forgiven. But whoever has been forgiven a little shows only a little love.'

"Now, I think that Jesus may have been taking a shot at me with that little remark, but I'm not sure. But then, Jesus really stepped out of bounds. He said to that woman, 'Your sins have been forgiven.'

"I don't care how holy a person claims to be. I don't even care if he can walk on water. There isn't anyone in the world who can claim to forgive sins. That's a matter for God and the high priests. From that moment on, I really had my doubts about this Jesus.

"Believe it or not, Jesus then had the gall to say to the woman, 'Your faith has saved you. Go in peace.' Can you believe it?

"That man comes into my house, as my guest, and starts complaining about how he has been treated. Olive oil and water are expensive. You just don't go around wasting that kind of stuff on strangers. And as for kissing him, why I didn't even know him that well. I mean, what could he expect! No ... I'm not ready for that kind of prophet to be mucking around in my house! No way!"

Poor Simon! He was expecting to make a mark on the world by having Jesus visit with him for dinner, and instead, we remember the visit by the woman who anointed the feet of Jesus with her tears and her perfume. If anything, we remember Simon for his lack of courtesy and wisdom by treating the Son of God so shabbily when Jesus was a guest in his home. I guess that should remind us to be gracious to all our guests because you never know who is going to be a guest that will be remembered.

But it is more than that. We see and hear the smug words of someone who assumed he had it made in the world, both materially and spiritually, and who was in reality out of touch with both worlds. The material things were too important. The spiritual things were lost in a haze of suppositions and preconceived attitudes that served to blind rather than to clarify.

We dare not look at Simon too closely, for if we do, we may discover a mirror reflection of ourselves. He was ready to judge the woman who came to minister to Jesus. He assumed that he was all right because he had knowledge and privilege. He was part of the establishment, the right group in the right place. There may have been a few flaws but nothing to be concerned about as far as he could see. Simon could not imagine why Jesus would treat him so badly in front of all his guests.

That is where we come in. I don't think that most of us really would imagine Jesus treating us so badly. We would see the pitfalls before they would occur. We are more sensitive, more cultured, more accepting than this Pharisee. We are Christians, after all. We know all about this love and forgiveness business. When we are part of the chosen people, how could we possibly be so insensitive? How could we possibly be so blind?

We know we are. It is the sin active in us, the desire to be right as often as possible, the ability to overlook the obvious and center in on our pride. We are used to being simply us, simply the self-centered creatures that Jesus warned us about being. We get to believing our own public relations stuff. We think that if we get a small handle on things everything will be all right.

So, when somebody new comes into the sanctuary, we give him or her the once-over and make our decisions. When people look like they won't fit in, we make sure that they don't. If they seem to be bearing pain or hurt, we move away just far enough to keep from making contact.

You see, that's the difference between Simon and the woman who comes to anoint Jesus. Simon does all the socially right things. He is an expert in being politically correct. He knows exactly what society expects, and he does it. He only puts himself on the line when he knows he won't have to step over it.

He welcomes Jesus, but doesn't offer the usual amenities. He stands in the presence of someone who seems to affect the crowds, but is wise enough to avoid making a commitment lest he should have to change his direction later on.

The woman who comes to his house is too outside the loop to worry about that problem. She sees in Jesus someone who has the power to make her different, to provide her with something she needs and desires more earnestly than society's approval. She feels a need to go and offer comfort and care to someone who deserves even more. One might say she was worshiping this itinerant preacher. And the preacher knew that.

Jesus was well aware of the woman, knew her need without her having to express it. He could sense her pain, sense her feelings of sinfulness and personal poverty. When she knelt to bathe his feet, he knew how genuine her tears were. He knew the cost of the precious perfume she used to anoint his feet. He knew her guilt and her total repentance. Jesus easily forgave all her sins.

But the one who needs to worry is not the woman who knelt before him, not the one who was told, "Your faith has saved you. Go in peace." The one who needs to worry is the one who has been forgiven little. To be forgiven a little bit is to be like those who are only a little bit dead. They miss the point. They are so caught up in being good that they fail to respond to the love that has been shown them. They do all the right things without meaning or purpose beyond doing the right things. It is as though their brains get turned off the moment they are needed most. Their hearts grow cold just at the point where they are being given the chance to burn bright with faith.

Can we expect all of our sins to be forgiven? Can we hope that Jesus would treat us so gently? Or are we simply Simon, assured of our goodness, blinded by what we think is good enough to get us in? Listen for the voice that says to you: "Your faith has saved you. Go in peace." If there is no comfort to be found in your listening, return again to the feet of Jesus and give back the love that has been given to you. See your sin and repent, for the mercy and grace of God is ready to pour upon you and set you free.

The Demons Within

Proper 7
(Pentecost 5)
Ordinary Time 12

Luke 8:26-39

Ours is an age that is filled with demons. There is more possession going on in the 1990s than has gone on in centuries. And the problem is that we don't want to mention it because demons are part of the mythical past. We in our scientific world do not believe in demons. That is because demons are powers that take away our control and leave us at the mercy of powers outside ourselves.

Now, I realize in saying this that there are those of you who are immediately thinking to yourselves, "Oh-oh! The pastor has just stepped off the deep end (again). He's turning into one of those religious cultists who see demons behind every tree and bush. Next he'll be warning us of the devil and his minions." Well, I want to put your minds at rest, at least a little, and invite you to hear me out before you put your brains into neutral and start thinking about the roast in the oven, the possibility of getting to the restaurant before the other churchgoers, or the golf game you gave up to come to church this morning.

I want to look at this story for what it is, to see how Jesus deals with something that makes us feel uncomfortable and to see how we might learn from this story. I think if we can translate some of what is in this text, we just might gain some useful tools in dealing with our world.

Jesus and his disciples had sailed across the Sea of Galilee to the territory of Gerasa. Gerasa was on the non-Jewish side of Galilee, where many Jews resided as strangers in a strange land. The first person he meets is an individual who is possessed by demons, a man who lives in the local cemetery for lack of a better place. He is feared by his neighbors, who have apparently tried to chain him up and keep him clothed for his own safety and that of the community.

He verbally assaults Jesus because, we are told by Luke, Jesus had ordered the evil spirits to leave the man. We are a little amazed by the fact that at this point Jesus has a discussion with the demons who possess the man. Jesus inquires about the name of the demon, who exclaims, "My name is Legion." The demons then beg Jesus not to banish them from the earth by sending them to the abyss, the way station for evil spirits that had to wait for their final punishment.

Jesus does not send them to that final destination; instead he decides to inflict them on a herd of pigs that happen to be nearby, reminding us once again that this is not Jewish territory. The infected pigs rush down to a nearby cliff and like an army of lemmings hurl themselves off into the lake to be drowned. The pig herders rush off to spread the news of what they have witnessed, and no doubt to report the loss of their pigs to the local authorities.

The local people race out to see for themselves what has happened, and discover Jesus in a congenial discussion with the man they knew to be just shy of a full load. The possessed man is sitting at the feet of Jesus, clothed and in his right mind. The demons are gone and things seem to be absolutely normal. And how does the crowd react? They react with fear.

They are told by eyewitnesses about how the healing occurred. They see that the man has been cured. And their appreciative response to the healing? They ask Jesus to hit the road. "Take your boat and go back where you came from! We don't want your kind around here."

The man who had been healed begged Jesus to allow him to go with them, but Jesus sent him away, telling him to go back home and tell what God had done for him. The last we hear of the man is that he is doing just that.

Now you see, the problem we have with this story is that we get caught up with the demons that appear in it. We start conjuring up all sorts of possibilities to explain the demons. Maybe they are these little supernatural creatures that look like gargoyles on the tops of medieval buildings. Maybe the man was suffering from seizures from some sort of medical malady. Maybe the man was prone to manic-depressive episodes that needed to be treated with medication. Maybe ... Maybe ... Maybe.

You see, we get caught in the story and perhaps miss the point. Jesus has the power to overcome the demons that infest our age. That is what Luke hoped to suggest in his repeating of this story. Remember that Luke was a physician, someone who, even with a very primitive understanding, still understood some things about the nature of human beings and illness. The Greeks were much more advanced in medical understandings than most other cultures of that time. They were aware of some of the physical and psychological problems that infested human beings. Their world-view included a mixture of science and myth. Some of their medical practices were still widely used until fairly recent times and some of their observations still inform medical understandings today. But Luke was also aware of demons and how they affected the world and people's reactions to those who had demons.

You would think that someone who had been healed of demon possession would have been the center of joy and celebration, and the one who was responsible for that healing would be treated with great respect and admiration. Instead, Jesus is run out of town. Healing someone with demons may not be the way to get praise and adoration.

When we hear the words "demon possession," many of us go back to the movie *The Exorcist*. We think of the sleepless nights and unspoken fears that were created by that film. Youth leaders back in the early '70s were deluged with teens who were terrified by nightmares filled with possessions and exorcisms. And when filmgoers discovered that the movie was based on a real situation, their fears were even greater. But that kind of demon possession only serves to make this story more distant, rather than helping us realize how many demons there are all around us.

You see, demons were the supernatural creatures that took control of an individual when they were not expecting it. They made individuals act in ways that were not acceptable. The individual was lost, and the demon became central in all that the individual did. That is why Jesus was able to speak with the demon that possessed this man. It was as though the individual wasn't even there. The man was an observer who could not participate in the world because the demon was in charge.

The demon was different than sin. You see, sin was what an individual did. It was disobedience to the will of God. A demon took control and in many ways, the individual was beyond the arena of sin. When you had a demon, you were not yourself. The demon and the self were in a constant struggle for control. In the case of the man that Jesus dealt with, the demon had already won. By chaining him up, his friends were actually doing him a favor. They were keeping the demon at bay.

Jesus stepped in and ended the demon's control. Perhaps that is why the local townsfolk were so afraid. Jesus was showing a power that was greater than the human world, greater than even the spiritual world. More than once, people asked, "Who is this that can control even demons?" They were pondering the possibility that Jesus might be more than human.

One of the things we need to deal with is that there are demons in our world. We speak of them all the time. Drug addiction is a demon. Addicts are always speaking of being possessed by the need for their chemical demons. Heroin, cocaine, crack, meth, call them what you will, but they are still "Legion" in the battle for human souls.

Power is a demon. And it not only affects individuals, people who must have power to prove their worth, be the power guns or political influence or the power of terror, but it also affects nations. Nations seek to control and maintain without a sense for the need of justice and mercy. And when that power rises to a crescendo, we see the results in a Hitler or the Klan, or other groups that thrive on hatred and fear. There are the skeletons of many burned-out churches in our land that testify to the demons of power.

Illness is a demon. With all our scientific expertise, you would think that we would be able to put away this demon, but we haven't. In all likelihood, that was the demon of the story we started with this morning. Mental illness is still just as powerful and divisive as ever. It comes as a curse, and we treat its victims as pariahs to be shunned and isolated. The word cancer can make us squirm with discomfort and fear. We run away rather than offering our support and care. AIDS is just as demonic as any other worldly creature. It ravages individuals while others seek to pretend it will go away if one ignores it long enough.

Greed is a demon, threatening to make us slaves of want. Avarice has always been one of the deadly sins, but today the desire to have and to hold is something that many in our society prize and encourage. Things are often more important than people, more important than faith.

As the scripture passage reminds us, the demons are legion. They enslave the individual, destroy the valuable, and release the very worst in us. The only way we can hope to cope with them is to come face to face with one who can drive the demons out and make us willing to sit at his feet, clothed and in our right minds.

And when that happens we need also to be aware of the fact that many of those around us will not be able to cope with our healing, for their fears are often as powerful as the demons that inhabit our world. For the demons are legion and the fears that we have about them are often just as powerful. They infest our world. But our hope is built on nothing less than Jesus Christ. With his presence and strength, we will drive the demons from our lives and our world and abide in the Kingdom of Heaven, now and forever. Amen.

To be sitting at the feet of Jesus is the only safe place to overcome the demons that affect us!

39

Ya Can't Make Me

Proper 8   *Luke 9:51-62*
Pentecost 6
Ordinary Time 13

One Sunday morning, a college student volunteered to help in worship by doing the children's sermon. She wanted to talk about how to be a friendly church, so after getting the children up front, she began by asking the question, "What would you do if a stranger came to our church?"

Immediately, one of the kindergartners raised his hand and said, "I'd run away and find my mom."

Another chimed in, "I'd say 'NO!' and go tell my Sunday School teacher!"

One after another the children told the young woman how they would avoid making contact with this stranger. She tried another tactic.

"Well, what would happen if a new child in town was visiting our church for the first time? Wouldn't you be nice to him?"

"Sure!" one of the children said. "But if he was a stranger, I wouldn't be nice to him!"

"What would happen if you were the stranger?" the young lady tried for the third time. You know that look of desperation you get on your face when you know what you're trying to do is going down the drain in a hurry? Well, that was the look she had on her face. "How would you like to be treated? Wouldn't you want them to smile at you and greet you like a friend?"

"Well, yes," replied one of the more thoughtful children, "but not if they were strangers!"

You see, what the young lady did not realize was that she had used a code word that those little children knew very well. Stranger Danger is a key program many communities are using to keep their children safe. They are warned over and over again to watch out for strangers. Strangers can be a real source of danger, a problem that has become a part of our modern society. Once those children heard the code word, our young lady was going to fight an uphill and losing battle. They were not going to let any stranger get near them, even if it was in the church.

I am sure you remember a time in your life when some parent or other adult warned you about dealing with people you don't know. Whether it was some transient begging for coins on a city street, or some con artist offering you an opportunity to win big money at a game of chance at a carnival, or some individual handing out some kind of tracts on a street corner, somebody probably told you to keep your distance and save your money.

There was a father and his family heading home from church on a lonely highway when they passed a car with its hood up, obviously in trouble. The owner of the car looked dirty and unshaven and was sitting on the ground before his rusty vehicle. His young son saw the man and said, "Daddy, aren't we going to help him?"

The father, who knew of the dangers of stopping to help strangers on a highway, said, "No, we have to get to the restaurant before they stop serving lunch."

The little boy continued, "But he looks like he could really use some help. Shouldn't we help?"

"We just don't have time," the father snapped back.

The boy then queried, "Is this kind of like the parable of the Good Samaritan that we studied this morning in Sunday School?"

Why are children so good at getting to the point of things?

We have a similar situation in this morning's Scripture lesson. Jesus was headed towards Jerusalem and was passing through a village in Samaria. An advance team of public relations workers was telling of his plans so that preparations could be made. But the people of this Samaritan village had no intentions of welcoming this Jewish evangelist on his way through town, heading to Jerusalem.

The disciples were stunned at the insulting attitude the people displayed. How dare they refuse to welcome Jesus! Here was the most revered religious leader of the day passing through their village, and they didn't even want him to stop. The disciples suggested that they call down a bolt of lightning from heaven to teach these ingrates a lesson. Jesus rebuked the disciples and headed for another village.

I suspect that those villagers in that Samaritan town had been told to be wary of strangers, especially Jewish strangers. There was no love lost between the Jews and the Samaritans. That was why the story of the Good Samaritan was so surprising to the listeners of Jesus when he told it. As far as the Jews were concerned, nothing good ever came out of Samaria. And the Samaritans felt the same way about the Jews. They probably figured that Jesus might use his visit to get in some kind of shot at the faithlessness of the Samaritans. This Jewish stranger was probably up to no good.

The villagers had been trained to "just say NO!" by someone. Avoid trouble before it began. Don't let those strangers get to you. And that approach is good for children and the naive. You never know when someone is going to bomb your village or blow up a bus. Someone might be out to kidnap you for some terrible reason. You always have to have your guard up.

The problem with learning to "just say no" is that you might just miss saying yes to a life-changing visitor. The people in that Samaritan village never knew what they missed when Jesus passed by. In some ways, it might have been better if the disciples had called fire down from heaven. Then, there would have been real evidence that something incredible had been missed. The way it happened, no one in the village could really be sure that they had missed something important. Jesus came to offer them life and they never even knew it.

It is like little children and vegetables; sometimes you can force them to take a bite, but you can't force them to like the stuff that's good for them. But the passage in Luke goes on. It moves from those who said, "No," to those who said, "Could you wait a minute?" Here, the answers are even harsher.

To the one man who wanted to follow wherever Jesus went, Jesus replied, "Foxes have holes, and birds have nests, but the Son of Man has no place to lie down and rest."

To the man who tells Jesus that he will follow as soon as he has buried his father, Jesus says, "Let the dead bury their own dead. You go and proclaim the kingdom of God."

And to the third man who asks to say farewell to those he will leave at home, Jesus says, "No one who puts his hand to the plow and looks back is fit for the kingdom of God."

We have three cases where it does not look good for the hesitant. Excuses will not make it when the call of Jesus sounds. And we are stuck with the same attitude that we found in the Samaritan village. They all keep saying, "Ya can't make me."

It is absolutely true. You cannot make someone love the Lord, or respond to God, or live a life of faith. It is something the individual has to decide. There has to be something within a person that recognizes the need for Jesus Christ in one's life before one can welcome him into one's village or home or heart. And being conditional about it, saying, "I'm ready but not just yet," will not create a situation of conditional salvation. It's a little like putting faith on layaway. It just is not the same as having the item in your possession.

We can put the obstacles in our own way that keep us from following Jesus. We can refuse to let him in because of our fears. We can avoid his presence by saying, "Not yet." We can even prevent a relationship from developing because we aren't ready to put away the past to deal with the future. Whatever the reason, the responsibility lies within our control.

What we need to remember is that when we are ready, Jesus is there for us to discover. He didn't destroy the Samaritan village because they refused to let him enter. He didn't forever ban those who had excuses when he called them. The door is always there. All we need do is go inside to discover the power and the grace of the one who has shown his love for us.

Were We Surprised!

Proper 9   *Luke 10:1-11, 16-20*
Pentecost 7
Ordinary Time 14

There is nothing like success to make you unsure of yourself. Perhaps the greatest obstacle to making a go of a project is the process of doing something so well that you never do anything else for fear of failure. If a writer makes it to the best-seller list the first time out, every novel to follow will be judged by the first. If a baseball player gets a home run the first time at bat, every time he or she comes up to the plate, the stands will be judging the performance in light of that first hit. If a movie director's first film is a box office smash, it's going to be hard to produce a second film that will do as well.

It sounds crazy, but it is true. It is safer and more assuring to work your way up than being a star from the moment you start. The young man was called into the boss' office to talk about his future with the company. "You've only been with us for six months, and already you've moved from the mail room, to office clerk, to the accounting department, to the head of sales and purchasing. That's an incredible rise in such a short time. I've asked you in to find out what your long-range objectives are so I can make adjustments with our management structure."

The young man began, "Well, within six more months I hope to be a vice president of this company, and with a little help, I'd like to purchase this entire operation and take over your office."

"Well, at least you're direct," said the startled president. "Do you really think you can replace me that easily? I've been at this a long time, you know, and experience counts for something. And what would you do with the company after you take over my office?"

"As I see it," the young man brashly went on, "I'd hold on to the company for a little while, wait for the market to drive the price up, and then, sell it and retire."

"But you're only 26!" the boss exclaimed. "What would you do with the rest of your life?"

"I've never really liked working that much. And besides, I'm good at relaxing."

"No, I don't think that you'll ever have enough money to buy this company in the near future. Not with an attitude like that, you won't!"

"Aw, come on, Dad! You'd only have to loan me the money for a short time," the young man replied.

We all know that success can go to our heads, and dealing with success can be just as debilitating as dealing with failure. Look at all the movie stars who have received incredible salaries who end up broke or addicted to drugs or alcohol as a result of their rise to stardom. We can look at the realm of sports and find the same kind of story.

In this morning's Scripture lesson, Jesus selects 72 men to go out in teams of two to begin the work of reaping the harvest of God's fields. He gives them specific instructions about how they should respond to the people they meet, what they should take, where they should go. He does not give them options. Rather, they get specific instructions; he even dictates what they should say and do. They will receive what is their due, but they are not to seek anything special. They are to carry nothing but the basics. They are to be single-minded in their thinking and their doing. They even know when they are to shake the dust off their feet when they have been rejected. In a sense, it sounds like a training session for door-to-door vacuum cleaner salesmen.

With this "by the book" marketing technique, they start off to prepare the way of the Lord. They are told as they leave Jesus' side, "Whoever listens to you listens to me. Whoever rejects you rejects me. And whoever rejects me rejects the one who sent me." It cannot get any simpler than that.

Luke records the return of the 72 by saying that they came back to Jesus in great joy. "Lord," they said, "even the demons obeyed us when we gave them a command in your name."

Jesus knew that they had followed his directions. "Satan fell from heaven like lightning. You have authority to overcome the power of the enemy. Nothing will hurt you. But don't get excited because evil spirits obey you. Be glad that your names have been recorded in heaven because of your work."

The 72 had been successful in their first attempt at spreading the gospel. They had conquered their fears and did what they were told. They were amazed that things had worked the way they had been told they would. That is usually the way it is with workers in God's vineyards.

The church financial committee had purchased a campaign package that promised great returns if the process was followed carefully. And for three years, it did well. Of course, those who ran the campaign made adjustments to the process. "People won't like that kind of approach." "Those letters are offensive and we can modify them here and there." "There are too many people required for this part of the program. We can probably get along with less."

Then, one year a high school student became a member of the committee, and ended up being the chairperson by default. Bob was handed the packet of materials and took them home to look at them. A couple of days later, he showed up at the pastor's office.

"According to the book, it says that we can get a minimum of a twenty percent increase in giving if we follow this program step-by-step. Do you think that's really possible?"

"I don't know for sure," the pastor replied, "but then again, nobody's ever followed the plan step-by-step." Buoyed by youthful enthusiasm, the young boy went back to the committee.

"We're going to do it all," Bob said. Not wanting to quash his enthusiasm, after a few half-hearted cautions, the committee agreed to do it his way. He was meticulous and sure. Every letter went out as planned. Schedules were followed. Dinners were served. Visitors went out trained and prepared.

When the pledge cards from members were returned, funding levels had increased 38 percent over the previous year. Three new mission projects in the church were fully funded. Giving to international mission was increased by one third and there was a reserve account set up for emergencies.

When he was asked how he did it, Bob would say, "I followed the book, and did just what it said to do. It wasn't really that hard. All I did was do what they said to do."

The next year, when the pledge drive came around, Bob had gone off to college. The committee, still amazed at their success the previous year, decided to use the campaign again, but they made a few changes. "People won't like that kind of approach." "Those letters are offensive and we can modify them here and there." "There are too many people required for this part of the program. We can probably get along with less." The pledge drive only provided an increase of a few dollars. "See, it only was a fluke last year. These campaigns never deliver what they promise," was the committee's response.

"Lord, even the demons obeyed us when we gave them a command in your name." Somehow, we in the church are willing to follow some of the directions most of the time. Perhaps it seems too difficult to follow all of the instructions. Perhaps we only want to do what is easiest. But I have a feeling that what we do most often is not really ask in Jesus' name and expect it to come true.

We respond in partial faith. We take our desires and try to make them God's. We strain out the gnat and swallow the camel. And then we wonder why we are unable to do what we have been commanded to do.

How many times have you really tried to share your faith with someone? How many times were you so anxious that you only partially shared it? How many times did you fear rejection and so decide that it just was not worth the effort or the embarrassment? Perhaps that is why Jesus sent them out in groups of twos. He knew that alone it would be too easy to back down if the going got rough, too threatening to follow through to the end. But with someone there to help and support us, who knows what might be possible? We might even be able to command evil spirits in the name of Jesus Christ and help bring in the harvest that has been prepared by God Almighty.

Who Was That Masked Man?

Proper 10   *Luke 10:25-37*
Pentecost 8
Ordinary Time 15

"**I just** knew it was going to be that kind of a day! I got started late. The people I was traveling with decided to go on without me. My donkey came up lame. And the beggar at the gate of the city warned me that the road to Jericho could be a dangerous place.

"But I had to go. I was already behind schedule, and you know how those things go. I was supposed to be in Tarsus by the end of the month. I hadn't seen my family in weeks. So, I did what I knew I shouldn't do and headed for Jericho. I wasn't more than a couple of miles out of town when I noticed that things seemed a little too quiet. Then, it was over almost as quickly as it had started. There were five or six of them. They took everything I had, the donkey, my money bag, even my cloak and sandals. And what's so silly — if they had asked, I would have given it to them. I think they thought I was dead when they left. I know I was unconscious.

"Society has become so violent. It's happening everywhere. Children don't respect their elders. People push and shove. City streets aren't even safe anymore. We're losing the old ways — no more manners, no respect. It's just hard to understand.

"Anyway, when I finally came to, I was so sore I couldn't even move. Blood had dried around my mouth and eyes from a cut on my forehead. The sun was so hot. I could hardly breathe. Then I heard footsteps. I thought it might be the thieves coming back to finish the job, but as I squinted up at the sun, I realized it was a priest heading up towards Jerusalem. He looked at me and just shook his head. I could hear him muttering something about the sins of the father being passed on to the sons and grandsons. He said a prayer as he passed. Then he mumbled something about having to stay pure for worship. He moved on.

"A little later, more footsteps. I moaned a little, thinking that it didn't matter whether it was help or the thieves. If it was the thieves, they could finish the job. If it was help, maybe they wouldn't think I was dead. As the footsteps got closer, I could see it was a Levite. He was probably on his way to work. My moan startled him. He looked like a mouse of a man. He looked me over like someone looking over a pile of old rags on the side of the road. He had the most pained face, somewhere between pity and disdain. At first, I thought he was going to help. He stayed over on the other side of the road, but squatted down low, looking at me carefully. Then he shrugged his shoulders, stood up, and said in a loud voice, 'Yea, though I walk through the shadow of the valley of death, I shall not fear, for you are with me,' and walked on.

"I had given up hope. The road had few travelers. I figured that two people in such a short time was about all I could expect. The day was really heating up. I knew that if I didn't get out of the sun, I would be dead before sunset. I understood why the two hadn't stopped. I don't know if I would have stopped if I had run across a similar situation.

"I was getting delirious when I thought I heard the hoofbeats of a donkey. My first thought was that it was my donkey returning. Then I heard a man's voice stopping the animal. By this time, my eyes were so swollen that I could not see who was there looking at me. But in a matter of minutes, I felt water being poured over my lips and face. A gentle hand began to wash away the dry blood. A blanket was stretched out over me, cutting off the burning rays of the sun.

"I felt my arms and legs being lifted up and bandaged, heard cloth being torn to make splints to secure my broken and battered bones. More water and more movement followed, and the blanket was wrapped gently around me. Then, I was being lifted up by strong arms, and I heard that voice again, steadying the donkey as I was placed upon it. Then, there was the slow, careful journey towards somewhere. I could not tell where. I lost consciousness again.

"When I awoke, my eyes were able to open, but I was in a small room, too dark to see much of anything. But I could hear voices out in the hall beyond the door of the room. 'Innkeeper, I don't know what his name is, but he needs to rest. Take care of him. Here is some money to care for him. I have to be on my way, but I will be returning in a week or so. If you will keep track of anything else you spend on him, I'll give you money to cover his care.'

"A few days later, I was up and around, sore as all get-out, but alive! I got word to my family so they wouldn't worry anymore. I found out from the innkeeper that the man who saved me was a Samaritan, a businessman like me who was just passing through when he found me.

"What's amazing is that I am a Jew. Jews and Samaritans don't get along very well, you know. He had no reason to stop and help. He could have felt justified in passing by, like the other two, but instead he stopped and helped. It's hard to figure.

"I don't even know his name. I'm tempted to hang around and see if I could meet him and thank him, but I'm going to have to get back to my family so I can finish up my healing. I've left a note with the innkeeper, expressing my gratitude, but that hardly seems to be enough. It's amazing! He treated me like family — no, even closer than that, like a brother! Yet I was a total stranger to him. All I can do is thank God that he came along when he did and that he was willing to go out of his way to help. It's nice to know there are some good Samaritans out there in the world. And I think I'm going to be a better Jew from now on.

"One of the things I learned is that having religion is no guarantee that it's going to affect your life. You can have faith, but if you don't live it out, something is missing. Faith has to be alive if it's going to be faith. There is something about the call to love that is more important than being able to follow the rules. I could be really mad at those two who passed me by that day, but I realize that if this hadn't happened to me, I would probably have reacted just like they did. I would have assumed that it was just God paying back a sinner for some awful sin.

"If I had seen a Samaritan lying by the side of the road, I probably would have thought to myself, 'Good! He probably deserved it.' Today, I could not ever think that. I know that if it is someone who needs help, that's all that counts. Sometimes, bad things happen to good people. All I know is that if I can help, I'm going to do it."

It is the story of the Lone Ranger set in ancient times. Someone who does good for no discernable reason except for the fact that there is good to be done. It is a story that has impact upon both Christians and non-Chrisitians, a model of sacrificial giving that goes beyond being a good neighbor and borders on sainthood.

What most of us would give to have a neighbor like the good Samaritan or be like that kind of a neighbor! And how easy it would be to do it. It would mean placing others ahead of self. It would mean loving our neighbors as much as we love ourselves. It would mean putting our Christian faith into action.

Perhaps the greatest question we have to ask is why we do not do it. Why do we fail to be good neighbors? Is it fear that stops us? Fear of rejection, fear of a loss of self, fear of disapproval by our friends for senseless caring, fear that we might get too involved? Probably, all these fears and more are part of why we can't become the good Samaritan.

Is it our lack of love that keeps us from being that kind of neighbor? Afraid that our love will run out if we use too much of it on strangers? Afraid that love will not keep us from being hurt?

Perhaps the greatest obstacle is the incredible cost that being that kind of a neighbor would require. We would have to lose our pretenses, have to give up our pride, need to realign our priorities and live the kind of faith that Jesus requires of us. That would put us in a very different relationship with the world around us. We would have to give up being right, and start being faithful.

Heed the words of Jesus as he speaks to the teacher of the Law, "Go, then, and do likewise."

Lectionary Preaching
After Pentecost

Virtually all pastors who make use of the sermons in this book will find their worship life and planning shaped by one of two lectionary series. Most mainline Protestant denominations, along with clergy of the Roman Catholic Church, have now approved — either for provisional or official use — the three-year Revised Common (Consensus) Lectionary. This family of denominations includes United Methodist, Presbyterian, United Church of Christ and Disciples of Christ. Recently the ELCA division of Lutheranism also began following the Revised Common Lectionary. This change has been reflected in the headings and scripture listings with each sermon in this book.

Roman Catholics and Lutheran divisions other than ELCA follow their own three-year cycle of texts. While there are divergences between the Revised Common and Roman Catholic/Lutheran systems, the gospel texts show striking parallels, with few text selections evidencing significant differences. Nearly all the gospel texts included in this book will, therefore, be applicable to worship and preaching planning for clergy following either lectionary.

A significant divergence does occur, however, in the method by which specific gospel texts are assigned to specific calendar days. The Revised Common and Roman Catholic Lectionaries accomplish this by counting backwards from Christ the King (Last Sunday after Pentecost), discarding "extra" texts from the front of the list: Lutherans (not using the Revised Common Lectionary) follow the opposite pattern, counting forward from The Holy Trinity, discarding "extra" texts at the end of the list.

The following index will aid the user of this book in matching the correct text to the correct Sunday during the Pentecost portion of the church year.

(Fixed dates do not pertain to Lutheran Lectionary)

| Fixed Date Lectionaries
Revised Common (including ELCA)
and Roman Catholic | Lutheran Lectionary
Lutheran |
| --- | --- |
| The Day of Pentecost | The Day of Pentecost |
| The Holy Trinity | The Holy Trinity |
| May 29-June 4 — Proper 4, Ordinary Time 9 | Pentecost 2 |
| June 5-11 — Proper 5, Ordinary Time 10 | Pentecost 3 |
| June 12-18 — Proper 6, Ordinary Time 11 | Pentecost 4 |

June 19-25 — Proper 7, Ordinary Time 12	Pentecost 5
June 26-July 2 — Proper 8, Ordinary Time 13	Pentecost 6
July 3-9 — Proper 9, Ordinary Time 14	Pentecost 7
July 10-16 — Proper 10, Ordinary Time 15	Pentecost 8
July 17-23 — Proper 11, Ordinary Time 16	Pentecost 9
July 24-30 — Proper 12, Ordinary Time 17	Pentecost 10
July 31-Aug. 6 — Proper 13, Ordinary Time 18	Pentecost 11
Aug. 7-13 — Proper 14, Ordinary Time 19	Pentecost 12
Aug. 14-20 — Proper 15, Ordinary Time 20	Pentecost 13
Aug. 21-27 — Proper 16, Ordinary Time 21	Pentecost 14
Aug. 28-Sept. 3 — Proper 17, Ordinary Time 22	Pentecost 15
Sept. 4-10 — Proper 18, Ordinary Time 23	Pentecost 16
Sept. 11-17 — Proper 19, Ordinary Time 24	Pentecost 17
Sept. 18-24 — Proper 20, Ordinary Time 25	Pentecost 18
Sept. 25-Oct. 1 — Proper 21, Ordinary Time 26	Pentecost 19
Oct. 2-8 — Proper 22, Ordinary Time 27	Pentecost 20
Oct. 9-15 — Proper 23, Ordinary Time 28	Pentecost 21
Oct. 16-22 — Proper 24, Ordinary Time 29	Pentecost 22
Oct. 23-29 — Proper 25, Ordinary Time 30	Pentecost 23
Oct. 30-Nov. 5 — Proper 26, Ordinary Time 31	Pentecost 24
Nov. 6-12 — Proper 27, Ordinary Time 32	Pentecost 25
Nov. 13-19 — Proper 28, Ordinary Time 33	Pentecost 26
	Pentecost 27
Nov. 20-26 — Christ the King	Christ the King

Reformation Day (or last Sunday in October) is October 31 (Revised Common, Lutheran)

All Saints' Day (or first Sunday in November) is November 1 (Revised Common, Lutheran, Roman Catholic)

Books In This Cycle C Series

Gospel Set
Sermons For Advent/Christmas/Epiphany
Deep Joy For A Shallow World
Richard A. Wing

Sermons For Lent/Easter
Taking The Risk Out Of Dying
Lee Griess

Sermons For Pentecost I
The Chain Of Command
Alexander H. Wales

Sermons For Pentecost II
All Stirred Up
Richard W. Patt

Sermons For Pentecost III
Good News Among The Rubble
J. Will Ormond

First Lesson Set
Sermons For Advent/Christmas/Epiphany
Where Is God In All This?
Tony Everett

Sermons For Lent/Easter
Returning To God
Douglas J. Deuel

Sermons For Pentecost I
How Long Will You Limp?
Carlyle Fielding Stewart, III

Sermons For Pentecost II
Lord, Send The Wind
James McLemore

Sermons For Pentecost III
Buying Swamp Land For God
Robert P. Hines, Jr.